Steve Austin
The Story of the Wrestler They Call "Stone Cold"

Ric Flair
The Story of the Wrestler They Call "The Nature Boy"

Bill Goldberg

Bret Hart
The Story of the Wrestler They Call "The Hitman"

The Story of the Wrestler They Call "Hollywood" Hulk Hogan

Kevin Nash

Dallas Page
The Story of the Wrestler They Call "Diamond" Dallas Page

Pro Wrestling's Greatest Tag Teams

Pro Wrestling's Greatest Wars

Pro Wrestling's Most Punishing Finishing Moves

The Story of the Wrestler They Call "The Rock"

Randy Savage
The Story of the Wrestler They Call "Macho Man"

The Story of the Wrestler They Call "Sting"

The Story of the Wrestler They Call "The Undertaker"

Jesse Ventura
The Story of the Wrestler They Call "The Body"

The Women of Pro Wrestling

CHELSEA HOUSE PUBLISHERS

Pro Wrestling's Most Punishing Finishing Moves

Kyle Alexander

Chelsea House Publishers
Philadelphia

Produced by Choptank Syndicate, Inc.

Editor and Picture Researcher: Mary Hull
Design and Production: Lisa Hochstein

CHELSEA HOUSE PUBLISHERS

Editor in Chief: Stephen Reginald
Production Manager: Pamela Loos
Art Director: Sara Davis
Director of Photography: Judy L. Hasday
Managing Editor: James D. Gallagher
Senior Production Editor: J. Christopher Higgins
Project Editor: Anne Hill
Cover Illustrator: Keith Trego

Cover Photos: Jeff Eisenberg Sports Photography

The Chelsea House World Wide Web site
address is http://www.chelseahouse.com

First Printing

1 3 5 7 9 8 6 4 2

Library of Congress Cataloging-in-Publication Data

Alexander, Kyle
    Wrestling's most punishing finishing moves / by Kyle Alexander
      p. cm.— (Pro wrestling legends)
    Includes bibliographical references and index.
    Summary: Examines the ways that professional wrestlers "finish off" their oppo-
nents inside the ring, describing specific holds and finishing maneuvers such as
the three-quarter facelock bulldog, the figure-four leglock, and the legdrop.
    ISBN 0-7910-5833-6 — ISBN 0-7910-5834-4 (pbk.)
    1. Wrestling holds—Juvenile literature. [1. Wrestling holds 2. Wrestling.]
I. Title. II. Series.

GV1196.4.H64 A44 2000
796.812— dc21

                                 00-020730

Contents

WHAT MAKES A
FINISHER A FINISHER?

T he two competitors are evenly matched. Each is a master of scientific wrestling, the art of holds and counterholds that is the specialty of amateur wrestlers, but which few professional wrestlers know how to utilize with any real expertise. Each is a capable brawler, willing to take the match into the sport's back alley, the area outside of the ring where the weapons of choice tend to be steel ring steps, metal ring barriers, and the occasional garbage can or ring bell.

For more than 20 minutes, the two competitors battle. They trade dropkicks, armbars, and leglocks. The battle spills out of the ring for a bit of brawling along the steel railing that separates the ringside area from the first row of fans. The match works its way back into the ring, where the contest continues. Neither wrestler holds a clear advantage over the other, until one competitor manages to maneuver the other into a face-to-face position that allows him to bend his opponent at the waist, wrap his arm around his neck and—WHAM!

What has just happened? The first wrestler has grabbed the second wrestler's head, and with split-second precision, sent his own body into a quick sit-down position on the canvas, driving the other man's forehead into the canvas and stunning him. In all likelihood, the first wrestler uses his free arm to

---

Hulk Hogan is famous for his legdrop finishing maneuver: first he throws a big boot to his opponent's head, then he knocks him off his feet with his powerful legdrop.

add some additional impact to the maneuver by slamming that arm into the opponent's back.

The pinfall comes quickly after this move, known as the DDT, is delivered.

That's the power of a good finishing maneuver. It provides the wrestler with a victory that is virtually instantaneous.

Not only can a good finishing maneuver be a wrestler's ticket to victory, in many cases, it can make a wrestler's career. Try to imagine Hulk Hogan without the big boot to the face followed by a legdrop. What kind of a wrestler might Rick Steiner be without the Frankensteiner? Could Bill Goldberg survive without the jackhammer? Or would The Undertaker be victorious without the piledriver? Consider how far Kevin Nash might have gone without the jackknife power bomb. And where would Ric Flair be without the figure-four leglock?

Yet a finishing maneuver is no easy ticket to victory. In the hands of one wrestler, a particular move can be a formidable weapon that brings a three-count pinfall every time. In the hands of another wrestler, that same move can have little or no effect. Why the difference? There are several reasons.

First and most importantly, the maneuver must fit the wrestler. For example, dozens of wrestlers use the DDT, but only a few have been able to fine-tune it into a consistently successful finishing move.

Jake "the Snake" Roberts is credited with having refined and popularized the DDT, and he uses it to almost incomparable effectiveness because it suits his personality. Roberts is the kind of wrestler who deserves his nickname, "the Snake." He likes to strike without warning like a cobra lying in wait for its prey. The DDT is a move that can strike without warning; like the most poisonous of snakes, it can have a very deadly effect. In Jake Roberts's case, the character of the move fits the character of the wrestler.

The DDT also fits Roberts's physical build. "The Snake" is 6' 5" and relatively slim at about 253 pounds, which means that when he delivers the DDT, he's doing so from a greater-than-average height, and with a build that allows him to put a quick "snap" on the move by hurling himself to the mat quickly. Those physical factors add impact to the move as well, making a difference similar to that between a whip being casually waved in the air or crisply snapped. Imagine a wrestler who is 5' 10" and 385 pounds trying to execute the DDT, and you can get an even better sense of how a wrestler's physical build affects his ability to execute the finishing maneuver.

A finishing maneuver's effectiveness can also maximized by the individual wrestler's strategic abilities inside the ring. If a wrestler falls into too predictable a pattern with the way he uses his finishing maneuver, then his opponents will design strategies to avoid that particular maneuver. A finishing maneuver is not of much use if a wrestler never gets the chance to use it. A wrestler has to be able to surprise his opponent with his finisher, so it helps if the move can be attempted from a variety of situations.

By the same token, if a wrestler gets too enthusiastic about his own finishing maneuver and tries to execute the move too early in a match, it may not work. The opponent might not

*Ric Rude has his
own version of
the DDT, which
he calls the "Rude
Awakening."*

be physically weakened enough for the maneuver to have its proper effect, in which case the
wrestler will have used his most effective
weapon to no avail.

If a wrestler's personal strategy includes
playing to the crowd or showing off for fans, it
is likely that the finishing maneuver will be
adversely affected. Many a wrestler has climbed
to the top turnbuckle in the hopes of executing
that picture-perfect sunset-flip, dropkick, or flying bodysplash, only to be tripped up by his

opponent (or his opponent's ally outside the ring) while acknowledging the cheers of the crowd.

When a finishing maneuver is successful, though, it is a thing of beauty, and an object of imitation.

Let's return to the DDT example. When Jake Roberts began using the DDT in the early 1980s, he was virtually the only one in the sport who counted it among his arsenal of physical weapons. Before long, however, other wrestlers took notice of Roberts's success with the DDT, and the move began to spread throughout the sport. Wrestlers like Michael Hayes and Jim Garvin began using the DDT. "Ravishing" Rick Rude developed his own variation called the "Rude Awakening." A little-known wrestler by the name of Dr. Isaac Yankem used a DDT variation that he called the "DDS"—yes, Dr. Yankem was a dentist.

Before long, more complex variations of the DDT began to emerge. Cactus Jack, now known as Mankind in the World Wrestling Federation (WWF), used a double-underhook DDT. Japanese sensation Jushin "Thunder" Liger perfected a DDT delivered from the top rope. Eddie Guerrero will sometimes execute a spinning DDT from the second rope, while Ultimo Dragon will execute a spinning DDT from the top rope, calling it a "tornado DDT."

The variations on the DDT illustrate how the sport of professional wrestling has developed over time. Through the years, wrestlers have become more fit, more agile, and more willing to risk their bodies in an attempt to score a victory over opponents who, in turn, are also more agile and physically fit.

As the stakes get higher in pro wrestling, the athletes' creativity level rises. Wrestlers take greater physical chances, telling themselves, "Well, if I can do this kind of a maneuver on the mat, maybe I can do it from the top rope and be even more effective, and create something for which there's no possible defense." Sometimes those experiments result in injury; other times, they mean that the sport has taken another step forward toward a new kind of wrestling.

Today, it's hard to imagine that a dropkick and a sleeperhold were once terrifying parts of a wrestler's repertoire. These moves are now so common, few wrestlers think twice about using them or being able to defend against them. Yet there was a time when a dropkick was as shocking to an opponent as an unprotected double-underhook piledriver is to the unfortunate opponents of Mitsuharu Misawa, who calls this move his "Tiger Driver."

Years from now, today's most complex wrestling moves may become as ordinary as a dropkick. Any successful new maneuver in the sport is sure to be copied, experimented with, refined, and taken to new levels. It's a fundamental part of what makes the sport so exciting, and what makes wrestling fascinating to fans.

On the following pages, you will be introduced to the finishing maneuvers (and the wrestlers) that have helped fuel the growth and popularity of professional wrestling for nearly a century. These are the finishing maneuvers that have turned wrestlers into superstars and launched championship title reigns and wars. These moves have made many careers. They are, however, presented with one very important warning: do not try these at home. Injuries happen often enough in the pro rings; these maneuvers in the hands of amateurs are like loaded weapons in the hands of children. Respect their power and leave them to the professionals.

SUPERSTAR SIGNATURES

2

Every wrestler has his favorite finishing maneuver, and in some cases a wrestler may have several finishing maneuvers in his repertoire. While a wrestler could change finishers frequently, choosing whatever he thought would work best on a particular opponent, most wrestlers change finishing moves only a few times throughout their careers, tending to use the move that best suits suits their physique and style at the time.

A younger wrestler might tend toward a speed-oriented move, while a heavier and more muscular wrestler will favor a power move.

Some wrestlers, though, seem to become synonymous with their finishing maneuvers. They make the move so popular, they are forever associated with it. Usually, this happens because they are so proficient at the move, no opponent can possibly design a defense for it. An effective finisher can do a lot to improve a wrestler's career. For the opponent of a wrestler with a strong finisher, it's not unlike preparing for a strong hurricane: you board up the windows and anchor down the loose furniture, but when the big wind comes, there's no stopping it, no matter what preparations you make.

Steve Austin prepares to execute his "Stone Cold stunner" on an unsuspecting Rocky Maivia.

STEVE AUSTIN'S "STONE COLD STUNNER"

This isn't a particularly complicated maneuver, but it's a stunningly effective one, especially the way "Stone Cold" Steve Austin executes it.

Technically, this move is called a "three-quarter facelock bulldog." Physically, what happens is this: with an opponent's head positioned just above his shoulder, Austin reaches back and grabs his foe around the head, locking the head into his own shoulder. Often, Stone Cold will reach back with his other arm and link his hands together, further preventing his opponent from being able to escape. Next, Austin falls into a sit-down position on the mat, channeling the full force of the impact through his own body and into his opponent's head. The transfer of energy is stunning, and the move rarely fails to subdue an opponent.

Several other wrestlers use the maneuver. Johnny Ace, credited by many with having used the move first, calls it the "Ace Crusher." Jimmy Cicero calls it the "Wisecrack," Hunter Hearst Helmsley calls it his "Pedigree Perfection," and Disco Inferno calls it the "Chart Buster." "Diamond" Dallas Page finishes a close second to Austin with this move, which in his hands is called the "Diamond Cutter," but it is clearly Stone Cold who has used the move to its greatest effectiveness.

RIC FLAIR'S FIGURE-FOUR LEGLOCK

In the annals of pro wrestling history, there have been few wrestler/maneuver combinations as inseparable as the "Nature Boy" and the figure-four. The original Nature Boy, 1960s wrestling legend Buddy Rogers, is often credited with having originated the hold. When Flair

took Rogers's nickname, he also adopted his signature move. But others trace the origin of the
figure-four to Eddie Graham and Paul Jones.
While there is some dispute as to who originated
this move, there is no question that Ric Flair
did a great deal to popularize it.

Ric Flair subdues Magnum T.A. with his signature figure-four leglock.

This is how Flair executes his figure-four
leglock hold. To place his opponent in the hold,
Flair first maneuvers the unlucky man onto his
back. Next he grabs one of the wrestler's feet
and performs a stepover toehold, then bends
the opponent's leg so that the foot is resting on
the other leg's kneecap, thus forming the char-
acteristic "4" pattern. With one leg already

entwined between his opponent's legs, Flair then falls to the mat and hooks his free leg over the foot of the bent leg.

It sounds complicated, and in fact the move results in quite a tangle of limbs (and quite a bit of pain, particularly on the kneecap), but an expert in the figure-four can apply the hold from start to finish in about two seconds. While

Like his brother, Bret, Owen Hart used a sharpshooter to master his opponents.

there is no true countermove for the figure-four, the hold can be reversed, though it takes enormous strength and determination on the part of the man placed in the hold.

Besides Flair, many wrestlers have used the figure-four leglock successfully over the years, including Jim Brunzell, Greg Valentine, Tully Blanchard, Austin Idol, Tito Santana, and Jeff Jarrett. It is Flair, however, who will forever be associated with the move and acknowledged as its master.

BRET HART'S "SHARPSHOOTER"

This move could also have been listed as "Sting's Scorpion Deathlock," as both men popularized it in the '80s and the '90s, and both men have used it to significant success. In truth, it probably should be called "Riki Choshu's Deathlock," after the Japanese superstar who originated the hold. Choshu taught it to Hiroshi Hase, who in turn taught it to Hart in the early 1980s. Even so, the move is most associated with "the Hitman" and the "Stinger."

To execute the hold, a wrestler must first maneuver an opponent onto his back. He then applies a standing double-grapevine by stepping through his opponents legs and crossing one leg over the top of the other, similar to the figure-four leglock, except that the ankle of one leg is trapped behind, not in front of, the knee. Once the hold is locked in, the wrestler turns his opponent on his stomach and uses leverage against the opponent. By arching his opponent's body and lowering himself into a squatting position, the wrestler who uses the sharpshooter brings incredible pressure to bear on the opponent's lower back.

The sharpshooter is so effective, it's been characterized as a hold that is impossible to break. Sting and Bret Hart's many victories attest to the move's effectiveness.

HULK HOGAN'S LEGDROP

It's almost absurd to list a legdrop as one of the sport's greatest finishing maneuvers. It's like listing hearing as one of the abilities a professional musician must have. The legdrop may be an elementary move, yet when used by certain wrestlers, it is transformed into a powerful technique.

Although he showed remarkable technical expertise in the ring early in his career, Hulk Hogan rose to international prominence primarily on his personality, power, and popularity, rather than his wrestling prowess. Hogan's opponents always seemed to be wrestling handicap matches against two foes: the "Hulkster" and his fans. Hogan's limitless popularity enabled him to score victories with a limited power-based repertoire. Indeed, he is the most successful kicker and puncher the sport has ever known.

Virtually every wrestler uses legdrops at some point during the course of a match, but Hogan's genius is in knowing when to use the legdrop. He almost always sets up the legdrop with a big boot to his already-pummeled opponent's head. Then, when the hapless foe collapses to the mat, Hogan takes one rebound off the ropes and launches his 300 pounds of muscle into the air.

WHAM!

The referee's three-count is almost an afterthought.

LEX LUGER'S "TORTURE RACK"

Prior to Lex Luger, the sport's biggest proponent of the backbreaker was probably Jesse Ventura, who enjoyed a nine-year career as a pro wrestler in the American Wrestling Association (AWA) and WWF before retiring from wrestling and later becoming governor of the state of Minnesota. The torture rack is Luger's variation on the backbreaker, a move that is not often used today, probably because it requires a rare combination of strength and control.

The backbreaker looks deceptively simple. First, the wrestler lifts his opponent as if he were executing a fireman's carry takedown, but instead he hoists him up onto his shoulders. The wrestler in the hold soon finds that the muscles and bones in his back and/or side (depending on which way he's facing) are stretched to their limit. The wrestler applying the hold then jumps up and down, causing jolting pains to course throughout his opponent's unfortunate body—hence the name of this move.

Only the strongest of wrestling's strongmen can execute the backbreaker properly, which explains why this became Luger's signature move. Luger is one of the strongest wrestlers in the sport today. It takes enormous power not only to lift a massive foe into position for the "torture rack," but also to control one's opponent while doing so. A savvy opponent can quickly shift his weight while being hoisted into the move (usually resulting in both men collapsing to the canvas), thereby countering the backbreaker before it's even been applied.

For Lex Luger, though, this is seldom a problem. He's so strong his opponents don't have a chance to apply the countermove and are forced to endure the torture rack or give in.

KEVIN NASH'S POWER BOMB

Popularized by Big Van Vader in the mid-1980s, the power bomb was actually first used by six-time National Wrestling Alliance (NWA) World champion and scientific wrestling legend Lou Thesz, who was of Nash's favorite wrestlers when he was a kid. Thesz, who debuted in 1932, enjoyed 936 consecutive wins between 1948 and 1955 and wrestled his last match in 1990 at the age of 74. Thesz invented the power bomb by accident when one of his piledrivers went wrong.

Indeed, the power bomb looks much like a piledriver at first. The wrestler executing the maneuver bends his opponent at the waist and locks his head between his knees. This is where the power bomb's similarity with the piledriver ends. Grabbing his opponent around the waist, the wrestler flips the opponent over and crashes his back, spine, shoulders and/or neck (depending on the angle of impact) into the mat.

The move is easy to use and devastating in its impact. As a result, it has become one of the most popular moves in professional wrestling. Dozens of wrestlers use the power bomb and there are all kinds of variations, including power bombs from the second and top ropes. Among the best practitioners of the power bomb are Sid Vicious, Scott Hall, Harlem Heat, Adam Bomb, Chris Benoit, Chris Candido, Dean Malenko, and Ahmed Johnson.

Kevin Nash is the biggest star to use the power bomb today. He's so adept at putting the full force of his 7' tall, 356-pound physique into

the move, in fact, that World Championship
Wrestling (WCW) banned it after Nash injured
the Big Show, who himself stands 7' 4" and
weighs 430 pounds.

Like the piledriver, which has been banned
from several wrestling federations because of
its tendency to cause serious head and neck
injuries, the power bomb is a particularly effective way of hurting an opponent, and therefore,
very dangerous.

3 THE POWER MOVES

onsider the elemental nature of pro wrestling: two men locked in physical combat with only their wits and their bodies as their weapons. Who will survive? All things being equal, the bigger of the two men will most often prevail. By its very nature, pro wrestling is a sport that tends to favor the powerful big man. Until the mid-1980s, a professional wrestler under 250 pounds was a rare sight.

Before the advent of acrobatic wrestling, which became popular in the mid-1980s, sure-footed powerful men ruled the ring. But a grappler doesn't always need to dazzle: a star who knows how to use his height, weight, and muscle to their best effectiveness can be both intimidating and successful.

It doesn't diminish the accomplishments of Andre the Giant to observe that at a height of 7' 5" and weight of more than 500 pounds, he was virtually immovable once he stepped over the ropes and into the ring. His sheer size made him one of the most formidable competitors the sport has ever known, and he knew how to use his size to rocket himself to superstardom. Similarly, Yokozuna parlayed a savvy knowledge of how to best utilize his 6' 4", 589-pound physique (he favored a bone-crunching move known as the "banzai splash") into a pair of WWF World titles in 1993.

A weakened Terry Funk attempts to roll out of the way before Sabu lands his splash.

The finishing maneuvers in this chapter are used by many wrestlers throughout the sport, but are used to greatest effectiveness by the sport's biggest men. In the hands of these mighty competitors, traditional moves and their variations take on a stunning new impact and almost always lead to decisive victories.

THE BEARHUG

It seems so simple: wrap your arms around an opponent and squeeze. In reality, there are two major variations of the bearhug. In one, the wrestler performing the move wraps his arms

Nikolai Koloff demonstrates a bearhug on "American Dream" Dusty Rhodes.

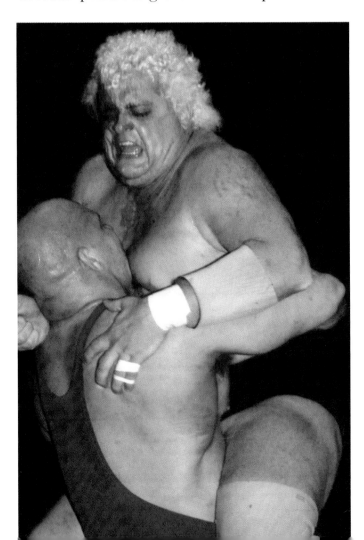

around his opponent at the small of his back. While squeezing him and applying a lifting motion, the wrestler on the offensive tucks his chin into his foe's chest for extra leverage, placing pressure on the defensive wrestler's lower spine. In the second variation of the bearhug, the offensive wrestler uses his own chest for leverage rather than his chin. The lifting motion in turn then places pressure on the defensive wrestler's ribs and the small of his back.

Perhaps because it looks so simple, and perhaps because today's wrestlers prefer flashier moves, the bearhug seems a relic of yesteryear. Bruno Sammartino used it to remarkable effectiveness during his two WWF World title reigns, which totaled nearly 11 years between 1963 and 1977. Ivan Koloff, Pampero Firpo, "Superstar" Billy Graham, Tony Atlas, Ken Patera, and Nikolai Volkoff all used the bearhug. They all had superior upper-body strength, the perfect criteria for being able to execute the bearhug to its fullest potential.

THE BULLDOG

Nobody's quite sure where the bulldog was born, but it was surely raised in Texas. That's where Texas wrestlers Dustin Rhodes and Barry and Kendall Windham learned and perfected this crowd-pleasing, opponent-beating move.

The bulldog is best applied in the heat of battle, slipped into the flow of match action in such a way that it catches one's opponent by surprise. To execute the move, a wrestler approaches his opponent from behind and slightly to one side, and wraps his arm around his foe's head so that the crook of his arm is firm against the base of the neck. As the wrestler grabs his opponent in this way (ideally with forward momentum working with him) he launches his own body forward and into a sit-down position on the canvas, thus driving his opponent's head into the mat.

The most devastating variation of the bull-dog was developed by Rick and Scott Steiner. In their version of the move, one man lifts the opponent in the air on his shoulders, enabling his partner to fly off the top rope and execute the bulldog from more than twice the conventional height. The added impact of the move is even more destructive.

THE CHOKE SLAM

Like many power finishers, the choke slam is essentially a straightforward and simple maneuver that allows a wrestler to capitalize on his innate strength. To perform the move, the offensive wrestler wraps one hand around his opponent's throat, then lifts him into the air and drives him into the mat back-first or shoulder-first, while maintaining the chokehold.

Hulk Hogan maintains his chokehold on Utah Jazz basketball star Karl Malone after chokeslamming him to the mat during their July 12, 1998, match.

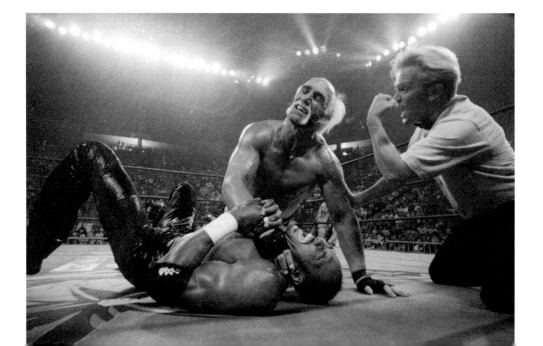

To imagine the impact of the hold, consider what it must feel like to have a powerful competitor like The Undertaker, the Big Show, Kane, or Scott Hall lift you and pound you into the mat. Now imagine that all the impact of that collision of canvas with flesh and bone is focused on your larynx.

In reality, the choke slam is an illegal maneuver, as all chokeholds are illegal in pro wrestling. However, the rules of most federations stipulate that before taking any action toward disqualification against a wrestler using an illegal hold, the referee give a three-count warning. That's more than enough time to deliver a well-executed choke slam.

THE CLOTHESLINE

The clothesline is a classic wrestling move, and for decades it has been one of the most widely used finishing maneuvers. Rick Steiner called it the "Steinerline." Ivan Koloff called it the "Russian sickle." Larry Hennig called it the "axe." They were all clotheslines.

This move is about as simple as it gets: a wrestler extends his arm and charges at his opponent, catching his foe in the throat and delivering a choking whiplash effect. It's a quick maneuver that carries high impact.

As with many simple maneuvers in wrestling, variations have developed over the years. Barry Windham developed a leaping clothesline that, like Hansen before him, he called the "lariat." Butch Reed, Sergeant Slaughter, and Brian Pillman took the clothesline to the air, executing the move off the top rope.

Perhaps the most brutal version of the clothesline was popularized by the Road Warriors. In

Hooking an arm around each opponent's head, Sergeant Slaughter uses a double-clothesline to great effectiveness.

their variation, Animal hoists the team's unfortunate foe on his shoulders, while Hawk launches himself from the top rope. This style of tag team clotheslining has also been utilized effectively by the Destruction Crew as the "wrecking ball," and Dan Kroffat and Doug Furnas, who dubbed it the "sky-high lariat."

THE JACKHAMMER

Bill Goldberg's remarkable rookie year winning streak from 1997 to 1998 owes a debt of gratitude to Dean Malenko. A major weapon in the rookie's campaign was the jackhammer, which Malenko originated by accident in 1993.

To execute the jackhammer a wrestler lifts his opponent into the air, as if he is about to deliver a vertical suplex. The vertical suplex is switched to a powerslam as the wrestler turns his body and leaps into the air, virtually "riding" his opponent into the mat.

The jackhammer is elegant in its power for several reasons. First, it's a maneuver that can surprise. Like a pitcher who follows two fast-balls with a changeup, a wrestler can follow two vertical suplexes with a jackhammer. The victim of the move is caught completely off-guard. In addition, the move is stunning. The full impact of two wrestlers hitting the canvas is focused on the wrestler sandwiched between the mat and his opponent. Finally, the maneuver places the offensive wrestler in perfect position to quickly score a pinfall; there's little additional maneuvering necessary to get into a three-count position.

The move was relatively new in the pantheon of the sport when Goldberg became successful with it. The jackhammer could become widely used, as future rookies adopt the move and develop their own variations.

THE PILEDRIVER

The piledriver ranks near the top on the list of effective power maneuvers used by the most wrestlers over the years.

Jerry "the King" Lawler built his career on the piledriver. "Mr. Wonderful" Paul Orndorff, Ron Garvin, Shawn Michaels, and Lex Luger have all used the piledriver. So have Don Muraco, Dallas Page, Chris Benoit, Kane, and Steve McMichael.

In the '90s, however, the resurgence of inter-est in the piledriver was thanks to one man: The Undertaker. This WWF megastar delivered a "tombstone piledriver" heard 'round the world at the 1991 Survivor Series. The victim of the move was Hulk Hogan. The payoff for Undertaker was the WWF World heavyweight title.

The piledriver is a simple move. A wrestler lifts his opponent vertically into the air, then falls into a sitting position, thus driving the wrestler's head into the mat. The effect of the piledriver is generally focused on the neck, and the vertical nature of the impact lends itself to inflicting nerve and spine injuries—which is

Jerry Lawler uses his favorite finishing maneuver—the piledriver—a move that has been banned by several federations because it is so dangerous.

why the piledriver also ranks near the top of the list of maneuvers that have been banned by most wrestling federations.

THE POWERSLAM

The powerslam is a demonstration of sheer brute force, a move designed for use by a wrestler with both significant upper body strength (so he can lift his opponent into the air) and significant size (so he can bring his full weight to bear on the impact of the move). When executing the powerslam, a wrestler will scoop up his opponent and, usually in one sweeping motion, slam him to the mat. In doing so, however, he will himself jump into the air so that, as with the jackhammer (itself a modified powerslam), he will "ride" his opponent to the mat. The foe is sandwiched between the wrestler and the canvas, absorbing impact from both sides.

The two main variations of the powerslam find the offensive wrestler either scooping and slamming in one liquid motion, or pausing after lifting one's opponent, then slamming him to the mat.

Junkyard Dog used the powerslam to tremendous effectiveness, calling it his "big thump." Other practitioners of the traditional powerslam include King Kong Bundy, Blackjack Mulligan, and Scott Norton.

THE SPLASH

The splash is a move traditionally used by the biggest of big men in the sport, like Jerry "Crusher" Blackwell, One Man Gang, Uncle Elmer, Typhoon, and Kamala. The bigger they are, the harder they fall—onto their hapless opponents.

There's not a lot of finesse or science to the move: the massive wrestler will, after weakening his opponent, hurl his own bulk into the air and come crashing down belly-first atop his prone victim.

The basic splash is favored by the biggest men for two reasons. It requires very little agility or skill, and it's about as decisive as it gets. There are not many wrestlers who can kick out from under the bulk of 350 or 400 pounds of wrestler, especially right after all that weight has just come crashing down on them.

Because of its simplicity, the splash is a move that invites variations, and there have been many over the years. Earthquake's running vertical splash, Vader's second-rope "Vader bomb" splash, and Yokozuna's second-rope "banzai splash" are three familiar examples. Two other variations—the flying bodypress and the moonsault—are favored mainly by smaller wrestlers because of the agility they require.

THE SUPLEX
The suplex is one of the meat-and-potatoes moves in pro wrestling. Virtually every wrestler uses it, and many use it superbly. In a suplex, one wrestler lifts the other into the air and deposits him to the mat. There are dozens of variations of the suplex. The belly-to-belly suplex, for example, finds both wrestlers facing each other. One wrestler wraps his arms around the other's waist, hoists him in the air, twists a half-turn, and deposits the man on the mat, subsequently landing on top of him in ideal position for making the pin attempt. Magnum T.A. built his short-lived career on the belly-to-belly. Shane Douglas executes an

excellent version of this move, while Rick Steiner does it from the top rope.

Other suplex variations include the belly-to-back suplex (in which the offensive wrestler stands behind his foe and executes the same basic move as above), the superplex (a top rope basic suplex), the side suplex, the snap-suplex, the vertical suplex, and the fisherman suplex. Many of these variations in turn have sub-variations. Among the belly-to-back variations, for example, there are the crossface, the half-nelson, the waistlock, the hammerlock, and so on. The basic takedown remains the same, but the way in which the offensive wrestler grabs the opponent can have subtle differences on the move's effectiveness and impact. Undoubtedly, the best current practitioner of the suplex and its many variations is Taz.

THE ACROBATIC MOVES

I n the mid-1980s, the sport of professional wrestling began to change. Riding a wave of unprecedented popularity spearheaded by the mainstream success of WWF megastar Hulk Hogan, pro wrestling was reaching more fans than ever before. For the first time in decades, pro wrestling returned to network television. All of a sudden, pro wrestling was hot, and all kinds of celebrities and rock stars began to appear around wrestling rings. This phenomenon, which became known as the rock 'n' wrestling connection, did a great deal to transform the sport and boost its mainstream appeal.

As the sport changed, the competitors themselves began to change, too. The average wrestler in the 1980s was a little bit younger, a lot more muscular, and significantly more athletic than the average wrestler in the 1950s or 1960s had been. By and large, those earlier wrestlers may have been better able to handle themselves in a street fight or an amateur wrestling ring, but the pros of the '80s were experts on discovering new ways to dazzle the fans. They took the sport to new heights— literally—as many of the new moves they introduced were aerial maneuvers.

Fans in the '80s were wowed by maneuvers that, once rare, were now becoming commonplace. Wrestlers who had grown

---

Executing his top-rope splash, Jimmy "Superfly" Snuka leaps from the ropes down to an unlucky opponent below.

up seeing competitors writhe around on the mat like they were engaged in a hyperactive game of Twister were now hurling their bodies through the air in even more impressive displays of athleticism. As wrestling became more popular to watch, wrestlers gave audiences more to look at. What these new wrestlers lacked in brute force they made up for with finesse, speed, and style. A perplexed opponent became an easier target for the pinfall.

The trend continued into the '90s as smaller wrestlers (who are typically better able to execute more complex acrobatic maneuvers) became more popular. Cruiserweight divisions were formalized with championships, and the lighter-weight wrestlers received prominent matches on high-profile television shows and pay-per-view events.

Though by no means a comprehensive listing, the six moves in this chapter represent significant steps toward the more acrobatic style pro wrestling has adopted over the past 20 years.

THE FLYING BODYPRESS

At its best, the flying bodypress is a stunning move. The two best practitioners of the flying bodypress in the 20th century may have been Rick "the Dragon" Steamboat and Mil Mascaras.

To execute the move, the wrestler first must weaken his opponent to such a degree that he is prone on the mat and virtually unable to move. This gives the wrestler on the offense the time needed to scale to the top turnbuckle in the corner and launch himself into the air, turning his body during flight just slightly so that upon making impact with his opponent, he

Ric Flair, bottom, manages to withstand a flying bodypress directed at him.

is in the perfect position to hook the leg and score the pin. If a wrestler doesn't weaken his foe enough, he's in trouble. The flying body-press is a very risky maneuver. It takes time to climb to the top turnbuckle and if an opponent comes to, he might simply roll out of the way. Another simple but highly effective countermove is to raise a knee into the midsection of the flying wrestler, stopping him cold as he lands.

Steamboat and Mascaras both executed the flying bodypress to perfection, and while in-flight, they were remarkable sights. Both possessed lean but powerful physiques, with significant upper-body strength that enabled them to withstand the impact of the maneuver.

Jimmy "Superfly" Snuka's finishing move was often called a flying bodypress, but in reality it was a top-rope splash. Snuka was unquestionably one of the best practitioners of that maneuver, which is often confused with the flying bodypress.

THE FRANKENSTEINER

Scott Steiner saw a move in amateur freestyle wrestling called the flying mata scissors, and he brought it to the pro ranks in the mid-1980s with a flourish. He dubbed it the "Frankensteiner," an apt name since this is a monster of a move.

The maneuver is best unleashed when a match is progressing at high speed. The wrestler doing the maneuver starts it off by whipping his opponent into the ropes. As the opponent rebounds, the wrestler leaps into the air and extends his legs in front of him toward his opponent. Wrapping his legs around his opponent's head, the wrestler must, in one swift and fluid motion, arch his body back and swing himself underneath his foe. This forces his opponent to leave his feet as his body is brought over and his head is driven into the canvas.

The move is not only stunningly effective—taking an opponent by surprise and dumping him on his head with incredible impact—it's also a guaranteed crowd-pleaser because it is so amazing to watch.

Steiner is the acknowledged master of the move that bears his name, but the success level of the maneuver, combined with its flashy nature, makes it a natural for others to adopt. Among the best practitioners of the Frankensteiner are Sabu, Jushin "Thunder" Liger, Ace Darling, Ken Shamrock, Juventud Guerrera, Mikey Whipwreck, and Doug Furnas.

THE HURACANRANA

Though it is often confused with the Frankensteiner, the huracanrana is a similar but significantly different maneuver. The huracanrana (roughly translated as "hurricane hold") usually begins when the wrestler doing the maneuver catapults his foe into the ropes and leaps into the air, extending his legs in front of him. Wrapping his legs around his opponent's head, as in the Frankensteiner, the wrestler arches his body back and swings himself underneath his foe and through his opponent's legs. This is where the similarities between the Frankensteiner and the huracanrana end. While the Frankensteiner is designed to drive an opponent's head into the canvas, the huracanrana is designed to roll an opponent into a tight pin attempt. Once the wrestler passes through his opponent's legs, he uses his arms to hook the opponent's legs. The combination of the arms pulling on the legs and the legscissors pulling on the head makes the three-count a virtual certainty.

In the springboard version of the huracanrana, the move is executed from the top rope following a leap to the rope from the ring apron. Either way, it's a very difficult maneuver to execute correctly. With one small error or misstep, the wrestler performing the move could be injured or crippled.

Japanese and Mexican wrestlers use the huracanrana widely. In the United States, the best huracanranas can be seen in the matches of Sabu and Rey Misterio Jr.

THE MOONSAULT

Legendary Japanese wrestler Tiger Mask originated the moonsault in 1981. The Great Muta popularized it several years later. But only when Big Van Vader began using it in WCW did the moonsault begin to receive its just due as a superb finishing maneuver.

The moonsault is fundamentally a splash or a flip with a twist. The wrestler executing the maneuver must, as with the flying bodypress, first weaken his opponent to a significant degree. With the opponent lying motionless on the canvas, the wrestler climbs to the top rope and performs a backflip, landing belly-first on the prone wrestler. The chest-to-chest positioning of the impact means that the wrestler executing the move is in an excellent position to score the pin.

The move is more punishing than a typical splash by virtue of the added rotation of the backward somersault. This full-body motion adds a whipping impact to the splash, not unlike the stinging effect of the snapping of a wet bath towel.

Both Tiger Mask and the Great Muta were schooled in highly acrobatic forms of pro wrestling, and the moonsault was one of many such aerial moves in their respective arsenals.

Big Van Vader, however, weighs 450 pounds. It is unusual for such a heavy wrestler to use so complex an aerial maneuver. When he first executed a moonsault, the wrestling world's collective mouth hung open in awe. The impact of the move was incredible when performed by men half Vader's weight, but it was positively astounding—not to mention deadly—when executed by the big man.

In anyone's hands, the moonsault is a move to be respected and feared.

THE SUPERKICK

It is impossible to know who first invented the superkick. Indeed, the move is not really a

Kabuki drives a superkick into Kamala the Ugandan Giant.

wrestling move at all. The superkick was actually borrowed from martial arts like karate and tae kwon, both of which use kicks to great effectiveness. The move may in fact be thousands of years old. It is, however, possible to trace the superkick's entry into professional wrestling: the wrestler known as the Great Kabuki first began utilizing the maneuver, also known as "standing savate kick," in the early 1980s.

Though the impact of the superkick is extremely powerful, the mechanics of the move are relatively straightforward. A wrestler will bend one knee up toward his own chest as he lowers his torso toward the mat. Extending his leg toward his opponent, the wrestler will snap his body weight so that it is focused on the extended foot, and kick out the leg so that the foot makes contact with his opponent's head. Usually, the foot will make contact with the jaw, delivering a resounding blow that throws an opponent off his feet.

As with a golf swing, the proper body speed and weight shift can make all the difference between a well-executed superkick and a sloppy superkick. Like a karate master using his hand to break a wooden board in two, the wrestler executing a superkick must think not about the contact point of the move, but instead focus through the impact of the move in order to maximize its effect. In other words, instead of imagining his foot making contact with his opponent's jaw, the wrestler must imagine his foot going through that jaw and beyond. As with all finishing moves, timing and positioning are also very important when using the superkick.

WWF superstar Shawn Michaels used the superkick very effectively on his competition. Other wrestlers who count the superkick among their strongest moves include Chris Adams, Tom Zenk, Brian Christopher, Ace Darling, Kenta Kobashi, and Savio Vega.

5 THE SUBMISSION MOVES

There's a big difference between a finishing move and a submission move. A finishing move is designed to weaken or stun an opponent to such a degree that scoring the three-count pinfall for the victory is inevitable. A submission move is designed to humiliate an opponent by putting him in so much pain he is forced to surrender and acknowledge the dominance of the victorious wrestler.

A wrestler who finishes a match with a submission move isn't just looking for a win, or even for a decisive win—he wants to establish his clear and undeniable superiority over the other competitor. He's looking for his opponent to "cry uncle!"

That's what submission moves are all about. When a wrestler catches an opponent in a submission move, the match is, in effect, halted and a new battle begins. How long can the offensive wrestler continue to maintain the hold? How long can the defensive wrestler continue to withstand the pain? If a submission hold is a good one, those questions are irrelevant. The wrestler placed in the hold will quickly signal to the referee to stop the match, preferring to add a loss to his record rather than sustain a major injury that could sideline him for weeks.

Using the strength in his fingers, "Hollywood" Hulk Hogan claws Ric "Nature Boy" Flair. Like many forms of live entertainment, wrestling matches are scripted, and even though wrestlers aren't supposed to hurt one another, they sometimes get injured and bleed.

Most submission holds are as old as the sport of wrestling itself, and their origins are lost in the mists of time. They have stood the important test of time, and while many of them are not flashy or pretty to look at, they are among the most successful moves the sport has ever seen or known.

Kerry Von Erich winces in pain as Ric Flair performs an abdominal stretch on him.

THE ABDOMINAL STRETCH

In an era that favors high-impact moves and high-flying aerial maneuvers, the abdominal

stretch may be a lost art. Look back to popular wrestling magazines of the early and mid-1980s, however, and you'll see the abdominal stretch depicted often. In those days, its greatest practitioners were Ric "Nature Boy" Flair, Rick "the Dragon" Steamboat, and Barry Windham. Japanese wrestling legend Antonio Inoki made excellent use of the abdominal stretch, while wrestlers like Toshiaki Kawada and Plum Mariko added a chinlock to the move for extra effectiveness.

To execute a classic abdominal stretch, the wrestler on the offensive must first maneuver himself behind his opponent while in a standing position. Grapevining his left leg over his opponent's left thigh, the wrestler then hooks his left foot behind the wrestler's left ankle.

The wrestler performing the move then slides his left arm underneath the opponent's right arm and behind his neck, bringing his right arm up and locking both hands together. By standing upright, straightening his body, and even arching backward a bit while extending the stomach forward, the wrestler can bring tremendous pressure to bear on his opponent's abdominal muscles.

One of the variations of this move is known as the chinlock abdominal stretch. In this version, the wrestler performing the stretch brings his locked hands underneath his opponent's chin, adding head and neck pain to the already considerable abdominal pressures being applied. Either way, it's a formidable maneuver that immobilizes a foe and, when properly applied, delivers constant and ever-increasing pain until the recipient is forced to submit to his opponent.

*Former UFC champ-
ion Ken Shamrock
subdues Roadog
with an anklelock
as the referee makes
the three-count.*

THE ANKLELOCK

If the anklelock doesn't sound like a very painful hold, you probably haven't seen it used by Ultimate Fighting Championship (UFC) veteran and WWF competitor Ken Shamrock.

The anklelock looks simple to apply, but it has its own unique complexities. The wrestler executing the move must first wrestle his opponent to the canvas. Once on the mat, the wrestler grabs one of his opponent's legs and forces him to roll over onto his stomach. With his opponent face down on the mat, the wrestler will then bend the leg at the knee and pull the entire leg up off the canvas. The wrestler in control will then use an overhand lock with his own arms and hands, immobilizing his opponent's ankle against his own chest and subsequently rotating his opponent's foot against the joint. If applied correctly, the move will increase in intensity until, quite literally, the ankle is broken.

The move may be concentrated on the ankle as a point of rotation, but the anklelock places excruciating pressures on the foot and the calf. Additional pain can be added to the move by bending the leg into a half-crab position.

THE BOSTON CRAB

The Boston crab was popular in the late 1970s and early 1980s the way Sting's scorpion

Former WWF heavy-weight champion Bob Backlund clutches Bret Hart as he prepares to execute the Boston crab.

deathlock and Bret Hart's sharpshooter are well-known today. It is a formidable submission hold that brings tremendous pain to the lower back. A wrestler must be very strong in order to execute the Boston crab, as it requires significant overpowering of one's opponent.

To start the maneuver, the wrestler must first weaken his opponent and get him on his back on the canvas. The wrestler in control then grabs his opponent's legs, one under each armpit, and locks his own hand underneath his foe's legs. By squeezing his hands and arms together, the wrestler on the offense keeps his opponent's ankles pressed against his own sides. By arching his back and lifting his arms, the wrestler is able to lift his opponent by the calves. In doing so, he steps over his opponent's body with one foot, keeping the other foot firmly in place and pivoting. Once he is standing over his foe, the wrestler on the offense bends his knees and leans backward slowly, gradually increasing the pressure on the lower back until the opponent locked in the move can stand it no more.

Pedro Morales, Rick Martel, and Nikolai Volkoff all used the Boston crab with great success. Stan Hansen's version of it was known as the "Brazos Valley backbreaker." Other noted practitioners of the move include Danny Davis and Jacques Rougeau.

THE CLAW

The claw is deceptively simple: spread the fingers, dig the hand into the opponent's flesh, and flex and squeeze the fingers. Those who have been placed in a clawhold by excellent practitioners of the move understand that it may seem simple, but it is incredibly painful and often results in bloodshed.

Consider a fitness fanatic who is always working with springed handgrips, or the strong man who shakes hands with the tightest squeeze you've ever felt, and you begin to get a sense of the potential of the clawhold. Now take that potential and meld to it a knowledge of nerve points in the face, the chest, the neck, or the stomach, and you begin to get a sense of the power and versatility of the claw.

However, the claw improperly applied is a dismal failure and will do nothing to stop an opponent.

The Von Erichs—Fritz, David, Kerry, Kevin, Mike, and Chris—all utilized the hold as they clawed their way to fame in Texas. Baron Von Raschke used the claw in the now-defunct American Wrestling Association (AWA), and Killer Kowalski's stomach claw was the stuff of which toughman legends were made. Other wrestlers who used the claw include Tiger Jeet Singh, the Sheik, Pampero Firpo, Barry Windham, Blackjack Mulligan, Rene Goulet, and the Crusher.

THE FULL NELSON

A lot of submission maneuvers become options when the wrestler looking for that perfect move possesses exceptional upper-body strength, but few are as effective as the full nelson.

Everybody seems to have done a full nelson to someone else at one point or another in their lives, but try to remember that this is not a move to be taken lightly. One false move, and the person placed in the hold could be crippled.

To execute the move, the wrestler performing the full nelson must first stand behind his

Sergeant Slaughter uses his cobra clutch, a type of sleeperhold, on Ric Flair. By placing pressure on the carotid artery, the sleeperhold restricts the flow of blood to the head and can cause the victim to pass out.

opponent. In a swift motion, he moves his arms underneath his opponent's arms, then locks his hands behind his opponent's neck. A fine point of maneuvers like the full nelson, which require the wrestler on the offense to lock his hands, is that in doing so, the fingers are never intertwined. Instead, four fingers are interlocked with four fingers. Intertwining the fingers individually (as if you were cracking your own knuckles) is a much weaker lock, and an open invitation to broken fingers.

Once a wrestler is in the full nelson, a few variations are possible. If the wrestler performing the move is taller than his opponent, he may use his upper-body strength to lift his opponent off the ground. On the other hand, if the wrestler performing the maneuver is particularly strong, he may choose to lift his opponent and swing him around in circles, a technique used to remarkable effectiveness by Ken Patera.

It's no surprise, then, that muscular wrestlers dominate the ranks of those who best utilize the full nelson. Hercules, Tony Atlas, and Billy Jack Haynes, like Patera, have shown the world that the full nelson is, indeed, a powerful maneuver.

THE SLEEPERHOLD

The sleeperhold has a long and storied history in pro wrestling. Wrestling's first sleeperhold was applied by Jim Londos in a match against Ray Steele on June 29, 1931. The 21,000 fans in attendance in New York's Yankee Stadium were shocked when, more than an hour into the match, Londos wrapped his arms around Steele's head in such a way that it brought pressure to bear on the carotid artery in the neck, thereby cutting off the flow of blood to the head. Steele slumped to the mat, and some spectators actually thought he was dead. The next day's newspapers were filled with speculation, which Londos answered by saying that it was "simply a new hold I've perfected which shuts off the jugular vein."

Some wrestlers who use the sleeperhold wrap one arm around the opponent's neck and drape the other arm over the top of the head.

Other wrestlers use a cross-face half-nelson to apply pressure to the side of the neck. All wrestlers who use the sleeper have found that it is an incredibly effective move, almost eerie in the way it elicits submission from the foe. The referee will check the wrestler in the hold by raising his arm, which will generally flop back toward the canvas. By most federation rules, three slumps of the arm back toward the mat signifies a submission on the part of the wrestler in the hold.

Sergeant Slaughter's infamous "cobra clutch" was actually a version of the sleeperhold. So, too, was Ted DiBiase's "million-dollar dream." Verne Gagne, "American Dream" Dusty Rhodes, Johnny Weaver, "Rowdy" Roddy Piper, Nick Bockwinkel, Jim "the Anvil" Neidhardt, and Jake "the Snake" Roberts are the most prominent among the dozens of wrestlers through the years who have made the sleeperhold famous by using it to their advantage.

Today, the most famous—or infamous—variation of the hold is the "dragon sleeper" popularized by Tatsumi Fujinami and Ultimo Dragon. With the dragon sleeper, Fujinami and Dragon utilize their upper arms more than their lower arms as the contact points for closing off the flow of blood to the head. Because of the greater strength in the upper arms and the varied angle of the hold, the "dragon sleeper" produces faster submission holds than the traditional sleeperhold.

THE TAZ-MISSION

In a 1999 poll of readers conducted by *Pro Wrestling Illustrated* magazine, the following question was asked: which submission hold is the best? Twenty-three percent of respondents replied, the "Taz-mission."

The Taz-mission is a move borrowed from the martial arts, primarily judo, where it is known as the "katahajimi." It gets its name from Extreme Championship Wrestling (ECW) star Taz, who first brought the move to American pro wrestling rings.

Taz's finishing move, the "Taz-mission," was voted one of the sport's best submission holds by the readers of Pro Wrestling Illustrated *in 1999.*

Once Taz has forced his opponent to the mat, he will wrap his legs around his foe in a bodyscissors, thus immobilizing the man by the torso. From there, Taz will apply a half-nelson to his opponent's head with one arm, while applying a judo choke just below the chin with the other arm. As if this is not enough, Taz will then apply varying force to the head with both arms, thereby cutting off air by blocking the windpipe.

Though the move is named after Taz, the Taz-mission (like the Frankensteiner before it) is spreading throughout the sport. Other wrestlers who utilize the painful hold include Tsyuyoshi Kousaka, Hans Nyman, Bas Rutten, and Gerard Gordeau.

The Taz-mission is a stunningly complex and brutally effective move. There is no known counter to it, and once applied, the submission often comes remarkably quickly. It's been said that the move is so effective, no wrestler has yet felt the full extent of the pain that the move is capable of producing.

Each wrestler has a signature finishing move tailored to suit their persona, and in many cases, as we have seen, this move is an adaptation on another very similar move. Though finishing moves fall in and out of fashion, they are just as often updated to suit modern audiences and new tastes. So when today's wrestlers apply their signature finishing maneuvers, they are more often than not paying homage to earlier wrestlers who used these same moves to their own ends.

It's part of the evolution of pro wrestling that new moves are created all the time: counters to existing moves lead to new moves to counter the counters, and so on. As that happens, the risks for these amazing athletes become higher, the action increases, and the dangers are greater than ever. This is good news for wrestling fans, as long as they remember to leave professional moves to the professionals.

Chronology

1931   Jim Londos applies what is acknowledged as wrestling's first sleeper-hold, in a match against Ray Steele at Yankee Stadium on June 29

1972   An NWA study reveals that victims of the piledriver have a 30 percent chance of a skull fracture and a 75 percent chance of a concussion

1976   Bruno Sammartino suffers a broken neck as the result of being hit by Stan Hansen's "lariat" clothesline on April 26

1979   In a Nature Boy vs. Nature Boy battle on July 8 in Greensboro, North Carolina, Ric Flair uses the figure-four leglock to defeat Buddy Rogers

1982   On June 28, Jimmy "Superfly" Snuka executes his Superfly splash off the top of the steel cage in New York's Madison Square Garden during a match against WWF World champion Bob Backlund

1996   Hulk Hogan experiences his first clean loss in more than six years when he succumbs to Roddy Piper's sleeperhold at WCW's Starrcade card on December 29

1997   Steve Austin's career is jeopardized when he suffers spinal shock syndrome after being the victim of Owen Hart's piledriver at the WWF's SummerSlam card on August 3

1998   The WCW executive committee bans the power bomb from all WCW competition; Buff Bagwell's career is jeopardized when he suffers spinal shock syndrome after receiving a top-rope bulldog from Rick Steiner on April 22

1999   Steve Austin battles the Rock at WrestleMania XV on March 28 in Philadelphia; each man survives the other's finishing maneuver, but Austin rebounds from two "Rock Bottoms" to capture the WWF World title

Further Reading

Inside Wrestling Extra: Fantastic Finishers. Ambler, Pennsylvania: London Publishing Co., 1998.

LeBell, Gene. *Pro Wrestling Finishing Holds.* Los Angeles: Pro Action Publishing, 1985.

Mysnyk, Mark, Barry Davis, and Brooks Simpson. *Winning Wrestling Moves.* Champaign, Illinois: Human Kinetics Publishers, 1999.

Sparks, Raymond E. *Wrestling Illustrated: An Instructional Guide.* New York: Ronald Press, 1960.

Sugar, Bert. *The Complete Idiot's Guide To Pro Wrestling.* New York: Macmillan Publishing Company, Inc., 1998.

Thomas, Art. *Recreational Wrestling.* New York: A.S. Barnes & Company, 1976.

Index

Photo Credits

Associated Press/Wide World Photos: p. 28; Jeff Eisenberg Sports Photography: pp. 2, 10, 18, 24, 36, 50, 51; David Fitzgerald: pp. 17, 26, 30, 32, 39, 43, 48, 54, 60; Howard Kernats Photography: p. 57; Sports Action: pp. 6, 14, 46.

KYLE ALEXANDER has been involved in the publication of professional wrestling magazines for more than a decade. His previously published volumes about professional wrestling include *The Story of the Wrestler They Call "Sting"* and *Bill Goldberg*. Over the past 10 years, he has made numerous appearances on radio and television, offering his unique perspective on the "sport of kings."